Growing Up Together

Margaret Becker

Photography by
Kathleen Francour

Harvest House Publishers
Eugene, Oregon

Author **Margaret Becker** is one of Christian music's most celebrated artists, with 11 albums that have earned 17 number-one songs, four Grammy nominations, and three Dove awards in her 14-year career. In 1998, Margaret broadened her artistry by authoring her debut collecion of essays, *With New Eyes*. In addition, she has been a contributing guest columnist for numerous magazines. Her regular column, "One More Thing," garnered her a prestigious EPA Literary Award. Margaret is also a much sought-after speaker at conferences and retreats across the country.

Kathleen Francour enjoyed a successful career in modeling and television commercials before picking up the camera. Her hand-tinted photography appears on a variety of products, including prints, gift bags, calendars, and in the book *Our Love Is Here to Stay*. She and her husband, Jim, live in Arizona.

Growing Up Together

Text Copyright © 2000 Margaret Becker
Published by Harvest House Publishers
Eugene, OR 97402

Library of Congress Cataloging-in-Publication Data

Becker, Margaret, 1959-

    Growing up together / Margaret Becker; photography by Kathleen Francour.

        p. cm.

    ISBN 0-7369-0224-4

    I. Brothers and Sisters. I. Title.

    BF723.S43 B43 2000   00-027798

    306.875'3--dc21

Design and production by Koechel Peterson & Associates, Minneapolis, Minnesota.

00 01 02 03 04 05 06 07 08 09 / IP / 10 9 8 7 6 5 4 3 2 1

You don't choose your family.

They are God's gift to you, as you are to them.

—Desmond Tutu

Contents

Introduction...6

Turn Around..8

The Bike 18

Silent Hero...20

Sisters in the Chase..26

The Exchange...32

Wild Ride...36

Perfect Sense..40

Introduction

*What greater thing is there for human souls than
to feel that they are joined for life—to be with
each other in silent unspeakable memories.*

—George Eliot

**With so much that separates
us in this world, it is comforting to**
remember that there are certain similarities we all share, universal
sentiments and experiences that continually bind us together as
one family.

Relationships between siblings are one of those binding
elements. Though our details may differ, it seems that the bond
between siblings has left a trail of notable experiences with the
vast majority of us, marking us with certain indelible impressions
that are oddly familiar when compared one to another.

The stories that follow highlight those impressions. They have
been written by several different people in response to a request I
made last year via my website, Maggieb.com, for stories about
sibling relationships.

It was a difficult task sorting through all the wonderful
submissions, but here you will find a sample of what is common
between all siblings, whether related by blood or just joined by the
universal cycle of growing up with other developing personalities
in close proximity.

I took the liberty of presenting each of the stories in the first
person, although only one of them is my own story. The body of
each submission is true to the author's original content.

I'd like to acknowledge Don M. Holman, Ericka Harvey, Mary
L. Nowacki, Jonathan Noel, and all the others who generously
shared their stories with us. This is their book, and I am delighted
to be a part of their telling.

—Margaret Becker

Turn Around

*There is a space within sisterhood for likeness and difference,
for the subtle differences that challenge and delight…*
— CHRISTINE DOWNING

When Mom sat me down that day, I knew it was something big.

She seemed nervous. I was hoping it wasn't like the time when she ran over our blind cat, Ginger, in the front driveway.

"Linda, I have something important to tell you," she began.

At least it was *important* and not *sad*, like the last time.

"Mommy's going to have a new baby." Although she was nervous, she couldn't hide her delight. "You're going to have a new baby brother or sister, honey!"

She reached out and cradled my cheek the way I remember her doing when my baby brother Joey was born. I hoped this arrival would be nothing like that. Joey was always getting into my stuff, and if he stuck out his tongue at me one more time, I mean it, I was gonna…

"Linda, what do you think about that, darlin'?" She searched my face for the answer.

"Make it a girl this time, okay, Mom? *Please?*" I blurted out, seeing visions of my headless Ken doll. Joey said he had lost it in the war with G.I. Joe—a token for the winning side.

Confusion played across my mom's face momentarily, but then the bask of "babydom" overcame her once again and she offered a loose promise. "I'll try, sweetheart. But you know that things like this are in God's hands. Let's hope it all works out, all right?"

I nodded, but I knew what she meant. I only had a few months of peace and quiet left. Ken wouldn't be the only decapitation victim in my toy box.

I wondered how it all worked. Did you *really* not get a choice? Did God *really* get the final say? And why would He send another Joey our way? We already had enough with just him. Surely if God could see all of this, He would spare me and get me a baby sister.

I dreamt about that for a moment. *A baby sister.* I would dress her, burp her, teach her how to clap hands. I'd *gladly* share my toys

with her. She wouldn't rip Ken's head off. She would understand that Ken is the *boyfriend*, not the *soldier*.

A few months passed, and we found ourselves waiting by the phone with my Aunt Sophie. Dad and Mom left for the hospital in the middle of the night unexpectedly. Aunt Sophie said the baby was coming, just to pray that everything went well—and "be still" in the meantime. She was looking at Joey in particular when she said it. He stuck out his tongue at me when her back was turned, as if *I'd* said it instead.

So I prayed. I prayed all the prayers we learned in children's church, and then I said one I made up after Mom first told me about the new baby:

Please, God, let me have a baby sister...

Please, God, let me have a baby sister...

Please, God, let me have a baby sister...

I repeated it over and over like that, the way I heard people at church do, under my breath, kind of like a whisper.

Seemed like forever before the phone rang, but when it did,

we all jumped. Aunt Sophie knocked the handset off the wall as she ran to get it. She seemed scared.

"Hello?" Her voice was shaky. "Yes…*really!* Oh, thank God! How long? Uh-huh. How big?"

My insides were spinning. *Please, God, let me have a baby sister… Please, God, let me have a baby sister…*

"I'll get them ready, and we'll be right down."

Aunt Sophie hung up the receiver and spun around just in time to see Joey sticking his tongue out at the phone. I was glad for it, too, because he was finally going to get it! But Aunt Sophie didn't seem to notice.

"Kids, go get washed up. We're going down to the hospital to see your new baby sister!"

My new baby sister? It worked!

She was red and wrinkled. Her eyes weren't even open as she lay in my mother's arms. A tiny tuft of brown hair barely covered her scalp. She didn't look like she was real. The only evidence that she was alive were the tiny movements of her jumper, pulsing up and down in slight increments.

"Would you like to hold her, Linda?" my mom offered. Tentatively, I shook my head yes. I truly did want to hold her, but she was so tiny. I didn't want to break her.

My dad lifted me onto the bed with Mom and settled me in. Even Joey was transfixed at the sight. Once in place, my mother gently handed the baby to my father, who in turn moved her towards my waiting arms.

Ever since Laura could remember, Carrie had been her little sister. First she had been a tiny baby, then she had been Baby Carrie, then she had been a clutcher and tagger, always asking "Why?" Now she was ten years old, old enough to be really a sister.

—LAURA INGALLS WILDER
The Long Winter

It's hard to say what it was like. As soon as she was next to my heart, I felt things I'd never felt while holding my own baby dolls. She was warm and soft—and heavy. Her pinched red face was almost without form. I could feel her tiny body breathing restfully. It felt peaceful and familiar, as if it had always been this way. She felt like an extension of me. It was almost magic.

From then on, my new sister Mandy was *my* baby the first two years of her life. I'm sure that Mom didn't mind. I walked her, fed her, helped change her. She was the best toy I ever had! Everything else didn't seem to matter.

I can still see her toothless grin. I made faces at her, tickled her, talked to her in a high-pitched voice. Sometimes I held her until my arms fell asleep.

It seemed that every day brought something new. We were inseparable. Even when I tried to get away from her, she'd just crawl after me. My name was one of the first things she learned how to say. It came out like, "Yeein-yuh."

For those years, I couldn't get enough of her. Then she turned two, and I turned ten, and everything changed.

At two, nothing was good in Mandy's world. "No" was the only word in her vocabulary. She had made the transformation from a "cuddle bug" to a "cry baby," as Joey often reminded her. She became a wild child who never seemed to leave me alone. I felt bad about it, but I just didn't want to be around her as much.

I was going through my own set of changes, too. My friends were becoming important to me. I wanted to spend more time with them, and that left less time for Mandy. I still loved her. I still played with her, but it just seemed like my days were being filled with other things, more so than before.

One day in particular stands out in my mind. It was a day of learning and change.

Mandy stood at the edge of our lawn as I mounted my Sting Ray bicycle. She insisted on knowing where I was going. It seemed silly to me, because even if I told her, she wouldn't understand. But I tried to explain anyway.

"I'm going to see my friends, Mandy. I'll be back soon."

"No!" she said sternly, as if she were the mom.

I was trying to be patient. I sometimes thought she just said that word because it was the one she could pronounce clearly. I don't think that she knew what it actually meant half the time, so I explained again.

"Yes, I am, Mandy. I have to go now, to see my friends. But

don't worry. I'll be back soon." I started to turn my bike around to leave.

"Noooo," she trembled.

I looked down at her. Her pointer finger was hooked on her bottom lip, and I could tell she was about to cry. *Great!* I thought. *She doesn't even know what she means. She's just not getting her way and that's what's making her cry. I won't feel guilty about it!* I kept turning and slowly began to push off. I heard her whimpering behind me.

"Yeeein-yuuuh…yeein-yuuuh…" She began to cry harder, and my name became louder and louder. I could usually tell when she was faking it. This was real. I turned around to see tears streaming down her face, her arms reaching out for me over the lawn's edge.

"Nooooo…Yeein-yuuuh-huh-huh!" the last of it deteriorating in the cries that come from the belly.

"I'll be back, Mandy," I called over my shoulder, but it didn't change the lump in my throat. There was something lonely about her cry, as if she were truly missing me. But I immediately dismissed it. She didn't know what she wanted. Still, I looked a few more times and pumped the pedals harder to escape the sound of her wails. I never did.

I think about that day a lot. I should have turned around— even if it was just to hug her and wipe her tears. I should have brought her in to Mom and got her mind off me. My friends could have waited another ten minutes. She was my sister, and she was

missing me. I just didn't see it. I regret it.

Mandy is a tall, beautiful young woman now. She is bright and witty, deep and soulful. As adults, we are both so similar in so many ways—just like I dreamed as a young girl while I prayed for her arrival. She has been my best friend, my confidante, my true sister. She calls me often just to talk, and sometimes to ask advice. I call her to see what's new, and sometimes just to hear her voice. We are there for each other. She is still one of my favorite things.

In July, Mandy stood in my driveway in Dallas as I packed up the last of my family's belongings into the car. My sons, Logan and Garret, gave their auntie a goodbye kiss. My husband idled the engine.

"Well," she started. But I was not listening.

How beautiful she is, I thought. A full three inches taller than me. So young and full of promise. *My baby sister.*

"Well," I said back. We smiled through our gathering tears.

She looked off to the south. "It's not so far. Only a five-hour drive." She shrugged one shoulder. I saw a little girl. "We'll see each other." It was almost a question, but not quite.

"Yes, we will." Mine was a sure statement. I swallowed hard. "Wish you were coming." My tears began to make their way down the side of my nose.

"Jury's still out, Lin. I could wind up there myself," she said bravely.

Visions of the front lawn came to mind, of a lonely two-year-old calling my name, her arms outstretched to me.

The same force that drew her into my arms the very first time inexplicably drew us together once again. I held her tight, the way I should have that day long ago. Fresh waves of regret and sadness overtook me, and I cried harder. I knew this was nothing like that, but it was raw nonetheless. Mandy cried, too.

Her mouth was muffled in my shirt when she offered, "Gonna miss you, Lin."

"You, too," was all I could eke out.

We held each other a while longer, until nobody was sobbing.

"All right, Mandy. I'll call you when we get in," I said, stepping away and wiping my eyes.

She bent down and gave a final wave to the boys and my husband through the car window. Then she turned to me. "Don't worry," she sarcastically offered as she wiped her face with both hands. "I won't embarrass you." She looked at the neighbor's houses.

I knew what she was talking about. "You're not going to run to the edge of the lawn and scream my name?"

We both giggled.

"Not this time," she said, as if I would have been lucky for her to do it.

"Too bad," I replied. "I'd turn around in a minute." I spoke softly, with all the love and apology that words can contain.

She released me with "I know."

And I would have.

The sisters went out to dinner full of their adventure, and when they were both full of the same subject, there were few dinner-parties that could stand up against them.

—E.M. FORSTER • *Howard's End*

"Jo, dear, I want to say one thing,
and then we'll put it by forever.

As I told you in my letter when I wrote that Amy had been so kind to me,

I never shall stop loving you; but the love is altered, and I have learned to

see that it is better as it is. Amy and you changed places in my heart, that's

all. I think it was meant to be so, and would have come about naturally,

if I had waited, as you tried to make me; but I never could be patient, and

so I got a heartache. I was a boy then, headstrong and violent; and it took

a hard lesson to show me my mistake. For it was one, Jo, as you said, and

I found it out, after making a fool of myself. Upon my word, I was so tumbled

up in my mind, at one time, that I didn't know which I loved best, you or

Amy, and tried to love both alike; but I couldn't, and when I saw her

in Switzerland, everything seemed to clear up all at once. You both

got into your right places, and I felt sure that it was well off with

the old love before it was on with the new; that I could

honestly share my heart between sister Jo and wife Amy,

and love them both dearly. Will you

believe it, and go back to the happy old times when we first knew one another?"

"I'll believe it, with all my heart, but, Teddy, we never can be boy and girl again: the happy old times can't come back, and we musn't expect it. We are man and woman now, with sober work to do, for playtime is over, and we must give up frolicking. I'm sure you feel this. I see the change in you, and you'll find it in me. I shall miss my boy, but I shall love the man as much, and admire him more, because he means to be what I hoped he would. We can't be little playmates any longer,

But we will be brother and sister, to love and help one another all our lives,

won't we, Laurie?"

He did not say a word, but took the hand she offered him, and laid his face down on it for a minute, feeling that out of the grave of a boyish passion, there had risen a beautiful, strong friendship to bless them both.

—Louisa May Alcott, Little Women

The Bike

He was the typical older brother, always pretending to look out for my best interests.

Glen would caution me as I sat on the lawn, season after season, watching him perform no-hands daredevil stunts, drag races, and bumper car matches on his battered old bike.

"Don't try this, Don," his voice would trail as he sped by. "You're too little, and you'll fall."

His warnings didn't help. The Christmas I was six, my one request of Santa was a new bike.

Christmas morning came, and we stumbled into the living room where, much to my confusion, I was greeted by *two* bikes. My parents lovingly looked on as I approached the tree. The first bike was a brand-new, burgundy classic two-wheeler with chrome handlebars and a leather seat. The other bike, a blue two-wheeler, looked extremely familiar—and with good reason. It was my brother's old bicycle with a few added features, including a new seat, wire baskets, and a horn.

As I eagerly approached the new burgundy bike, I noticed a tag hanging from the handlebars. My heart sank when I read it: "To Glen, From Santa." One look at the tag on my brother's bike confirmed my fears: "To Don, From Santa." *I* was getting my brother's *hand-me-down* and he was getting the *new* bike. I glanced at my parents, who seemed confused by my disappointment. They didn't seem to notice my brother's sheer delight.

Discreetly, Mom and Dad made their way to where I stood and searched for the source of my angst. When they saw the tags, they were undoubtedly more surprised about the discovery than I. They exchanged looks of recognition and suppressed laughter. The tags came off and some comment was made about how tired Santa must have been when he delivered the gifts last night because he got the tags wrong. This last part of the explanation was directed at my gloating brother.

My brother, Glen. Can you believe he grew up to be a minister?

Silent Hero

Our relationship was simple as breath, complex as circulation.
She was only the first person I could tell the truth to.

—ELIZABETH FISHEL

*W*e were opposites from the start. I refused to shut up. My brother Pete refused to talk. Only two years separated us, but his reluctance to speak kept me outside his world.

I was six when Pete went to the first doctor. At four, most kids are chatterboxes, but my brother was silent. It was a curious thing to me, because somehow I understood him in spite of it. I understood when he wanted to play. I understood when he needed me to help him reach something. I understood when no amount of coaxing would make him speak.

Our family breathed a collective sigh of relief when the reason for Pete's silence arrived. My brother had a speech impediment. He knew how to talk, but the impediment made him shy.

Pete doesn't have to be shy around me, I decided. And so I singularly resolved to help him overcome his fear of speaking aloud.

How patient he was with my efforts! Afternoons were our lesson times, and I took my job as the "teacher" seriously. I tried to get him to recite his ABC's. I read stories to him and quizzed him on the plot. I asked him to read me the numbers on the television dial. Nothing worked.

Quite by accident one Saturday, I discovered something that signaled progress. We were playing hide and seek, Pete's favorite game—especially when it was his turn to find me. While Pete covered his head with his forearm and began the silent count to twenty, I scrambled for a place to hide. I paused for a moment, considering my options. It was then that I heard something that sounded like a tiny whisper. "…two…three…four…" I was shocked. It wasn't very loud, but Pete *was* counting, whispering the numbers to himself.

It was the start I needed. We played hide and seek every day for weeks, until one day I ran out of good hiding places. On that day the game commenced as usual. I waited for Pete to duck his head and start reciting the numbers.

He has also brotherly pride, which with some brotherly affection, makes him a very kind and careful guardian of his sister; and you will hear him generally cried up as the most attentive and best of brothers.

—JANE AUSTEN • *Pride and Prejudice*

Where should I go? I needed some new place to hide to keep him interested in the game. It was getting too easy for him. I'd hid everywhere around the house. We'd explored every nook and cranny except…*no!* It was unthinkable.

"…fourteen…um…twelve…thirteen…" The tiny whispers continued on. Twenty was coming up soon. I glanced up the stairs and made a wild decision.

I flew up the first set of steps on all fours, quietly, like a cat. My heart was pounding, but not from the effort. I rounded the second set with mounting fear. I was headed to the one place I knew Pete wouldn't look, the one place we'd *never* include in our game. *The monster closet.*

The monster closet was big—huge, in fact—and divided into two sections. It was also very dark. The one source of light was a bare bulb with a string attached that dangled from the ceiling. But the string was much too high for me to reach.

The monster closet was also deep. No matter how hard you dared to stare, you couldn't ever seem to make out the back wall. Truth was, if you stared too long, things moved in wavy phantomlike dances. Sometimes I saw white ghost eyes peering back at me. I hated that closet.

And worse yet, it was in my bedroom. For the first part of my life, I made sure to make a wide arc around it every time I had to walk near it. Monsters can move quickly, and at any given moment they might snatch me in.

Fortunately, I didn't have to look *in* the closet but four times a year, when my mother would change out her wardrobe and pack away the last season's clothes. Even with Mom leading the charge, though, I still felt like it was dangerous to linger too long. But I took the opportunity when Mom was near to stare the monsters down, to show them I was not alone.

All those years, I wasn't sure what the phantoms would do if they got their way, I just knew that they'd *get* me—and that was enough. I hated that closet, and my whole family knew it, too.

I rounded the bend in my room, and I heard Pete begin the trek up the stairs. My heart was pounding so hard that it felt like it was on the outside of my skin. I thought about just diving under the bed, but I knew that would be the first place Pete would look. Throwing caution to the wind, I took small, swift steps to the closet and backed myself in so that I wouldn't have to see anything. I left the door slightly ajar to let some light inside. I knew that monsters didn't like light, and besides, that was my *real* life out there in the room, cozy and safe. I could return to it anytime as long as I could see it.

I heard the soft patter of Pete's feet and saw him run by my room. I was sure that he'd seen me there in the light of the door, but he continued on down the hall. Feeling a little bit braver as I heard him moving to check all the usual hiding places, I decided to make the game a little harder for him. So I reached forward and gave the door a soft tug to let less light in.

It shut. Fully. With no handle on the inside.

I felt the air rush out of me. My skin went cold. The hairs on the back of my neck prickled. I turned my head slightly to the side, expecting to see the white eyes shining in the darkness. Then I heard Pete approach the outside of the closet. Not wanting him to *feel* my panic, I tried to control my voice.

"Pete, open the door."

He sensed my fear. I could hear him frantically trying to reach up and undo the latch, but he was too small.

"It's okay, Pete." I tried to steady my voice. "Mommy's in the basement doing the laundry. Go get her! Hurry!"

His sneakers slapped the hardwood as he took off. I strained to hear him finish the second set of steps when a worse fear took hold of me. Panic flushed my face.

Oh, no! He'll go to Mom, but he won't be able to tell her where I am!

I turned my head quickly to see if the monsters knew my vulnerability, flying into a fury of motion when I was sure I saw the soulless eyes staring back through the darkness. Kicking the door and screaming at the top of my lungs, I wailed until I almost lost consciousness. It was then that I heard two sets of footsteps approaching the closet.

"Tell me again, Pete! Let Rosie hear what you told me." I heard my mother's voice, choked with emotion. I strained at the door and heard a sound I'd never heard before.

"Rosie's in the closet with the monsters! She can't get out! Get her out!" Pete was crying, but through his sobs he'd managed to tell Mom what had happened. It was the most I'd ever heard him say.

The latch flew up and Pete rushed forward to hug my neck. All three of us stood there crying. Mom and I, laughing with joy.

Pete, obviously shocked at the sound of his own voice, cried the last of his tears as he slowly allowed the comfort of the rescue to take hold.

Afterwards, I took Pete to a store in our neighborhood and bought him a popsicle. It seemed a fitting reward for a hero.

We talked about what had happened. Between raspberry licks, he asked me if I'd been scared. I told him yes. I asked him if he'd been scared. He was.

The first words spoken began the exchange I'd longed for over the past year.

My brother's little boy face, still marked by the tracks of his tears, stood like a knight in shining armor on the sidewalk—once frightened by the sound of his own voice, now brave enough to shout into the monster closet.

Strong enough to overcome them all.

A hero indeed.

In a few minutes, Jo bounced in, laid herself on the sofa, and affected to read.

"Have you anything interesting there?" asked Meg with condescension.

"Nothing but a story; won't amount to much, I guess," returned Jo, carefully keeping the name of the paper out of sight.

"You'd better read it aloud; that will amuse us and keep you out of mischief," said Amy in her most grown-up tone.

"What's the name?" asked Beth, wondering why Jo kept her face behind the sheet.

"The Rival Painters."

"That sounds well; read it," said Meg.

With a loud "Hem!" and a long breath, Jo began to read very fast. The girls listened with interest, for the tale was romantic, and somewhat pathetic, as most of the characters died in the end.

"I like that about the splendid picture," was Amy's approving remark, as Jo paused.

"I prefer the lovering part. Viola and Angelo are two of our favorite names, isn't that queer?" said Meg, wiping her eyes, for the "lovering part" was tragical.

"Who wrote it?" asked Beth, who had caught a glimpse of Jo's face.

The reader suddenly sat up, cast away the paper, displaying a flushed countenance, and with a funny mixture of solemnity and excitement replied in a loud voice, "Your sister."

"You?" cried Meg, dropping her work.

"It's very good," said Amy critically.

"I knew it! I knew it! Oh, my Jo, I am so proud!" And Beth ran to hug her sister and exult over this splendid success.

–Louisa May Alcott, Little Women

Sisters in the Chase

*A sister can be seen as someone who is both ourselves
and very much not ourselves—a special kind of double.*

—TONI MORRISON

Although I'm not sure how I first understood it, I knew that my developmentally disabled sister Janie was fragile, and that in all things she must come first.

I think I sensed it innately as a child because perhaps as children we're more open to those merciful instincts that play across our consciences. Or maybe it's just that I saw the way other people treated her, like a beautiful porcelain doll, valuable and lovely, but not for play.

Even as a child, I strained with all my senses to feel what Janie felt. I wanted to see through her eyes. I wanted to know her beyond what she could tell me. Her disability had left her without speech, so my task of "knowing" became wholly centered in nuance. I tried to unravel every mysterious expression, every response or lack of one to the surrounding world. I watched intently, from my emotions outward, trying to trace the edges of her being. I wanted

to know her the way I knew my other siblings: what made her angry, what made her smile, what were her limits of tolerance. And once I learned them, I wanted to protect them, cater to them, and in some younger sister way, perhaps push them. Not in the way most kids do, out of spite, but rather with affection. I wanted to hug her, stroke her silky black hair, hold her hand, and skip down the driveway…all seemingly against her will.

Janie seemed unaware of me most of the time, or perhaps just indifferent. I'm sure that some of it had to do with the fact that I was the "new kid" in her world—draining all the attention she had become accustomed to. That was reason enough. But it was more than that. She was refused entry into the outside world because she didn't have the abilities to communicate with it. She retreated inward, searching for distractions and stimulus, reaching for what we all take for granted: the small evidences of being alive. I was part of the outside, an unwilling exile—but undaunted in my

For there is no friend like a sister
In calm or stormy weather;
To cheer one on the tedious way,
To fetch one if one goes astray,
To lift one if one totters down,
To strengthen whilst one stands.
—CHRISTINA ROSSETTI

youthful energy. I would try with all the resources I had.

From the beginning, Janie's delight was my delight. I wanted her to be happy. It was the most direct way to get into her world—making her content. I started with what I knew: the things that made me happy, like being first. I learned early how to stand back when we'd hear the rumble of my father's jeep in the evening. I knew to allow her to run ahead of me when he emerged from behind the squeaky green door, black lunch box in hand. After a long day's work, he smelled of wind and of sweat dried to a salt. And although I believe my father was dreaming of an ice-cold beer and a long shower, his attentions lay solely on us in those first moments of his free evening.

It was against the backdrop of my father's half-crouched body that I remember seeing a smile slowly emerge on Janie's face. Sometimes it was her only smile of the day.

On those nights my father played a friendly stalker, his Frankensteinesque strides making me flush with nervous anticipation. Shifting from foot to foot, Janie and I would jitter and dance with delight, our hands up to our faces. Fingers spread wide,

we hid our tangled smiles. We awaited the familiar danger of the chase that was coming.

My father's growls were punctuated with laughter as he lumbered toward Janie. Her guttural giggling trailed behind her as she dragged her feet, always remaining close enough to catch. Several trips around the yard later, my father would snatch her into his arms and rub the tiny bristles of his five o'clock shadow against her creamy white Irish skin. Squirming happily in her yellow sunsuit, she'd wriggle away with a backward glance and assume her "catch me" stance, ready for more. This was a ritual, and when Janie was through, I was next.

We understood it. We reveled in it. We never acknowledged it to one another, but I knew we both felt it.

Sisters, both of us in our sunsuits; hers was always immaculate, mine always smeared with the long, brown dusty strokes of Long Island soil, the evidence of tomboy games and hide and seek. We were sisters in the chase there in our tiny suburban front yard, sisters both bound and separated by genetics and circumstance. There where the friendly stalker made our laughter resound wildly through the streets, blood reigned and we were one.

Though utterly unlike in character,

the twins got on remarkably well

together, and seldom quarreled more

than thrice a day. Of course, Demi

tyrannized over Daisy, and gallantly

defended her from every other aggressor,

while Daisy made a galley slave of

herself, and adored her brother as

the one perfect being in the world.
—Louisa May Alcott, Little Women

The Exchange

Call it a clan, call it a network, call it a tribe, call it a family.
Whatever you call it, whoever you are, you need one.

—JANE HOWARD

There were way too many of us, as I look back on it now. I can't imagine how my parents did it. With eight kids under the same roof, the regular procedures of living took on an abbreviated form. From time spent in the bathroom to the milk, everything in measure and moderation. Of course, there were some in the family who took advantage— sneaking extra Cheerios, taking too long in the shower, having two helpings of cake—but for the most part, we understood that whereas most families were a small group, we were a small *country*. And being a small country meant living with small compromises.

As people tend to do in large groups, we divided into several sets as we grew. I was in one set called "the little guys." I was the youngest, and in my clan were Paul and Lisa, both slightly older than me. Although we were as different as kids can be, as "the little guys" we generally stuck together and stayed to ourselves. We were closer to one another than we were to the rest of the family—still

are. We needed our collective presence in order to exert any kind of power in the chaos.

The task of raising eight kids is difficult enough, but remembering preferences, likes and dislikes, even things as important as birthdays, was hard for my parents. At times, they even forgot our names. My mom, in her frustration, would just run down the entire list when someone was in trouble. She knew that eventually the right name would be bellowed and the appropriate body in front of her would quake.

Our house was a continual stream of voices and activities, an erupting volcano of developing personalities, bouncing off one another like atoms over heat. Crazy and disjointed most every day, except for one—Christmas.

Christmas was the single day when a sense of unity prevailed. Unlike the rest of my family life, it seemed that on this day we were working as one body, all in agreement somehow, bound by the

Sisters make the real conversations…not the saying

but the never needing to say is what counts.

—MARGARET LEE RUNBECK

celebratory mood. Even though there were differences and difficulties throughout the year, somehow on that holiday the momentum of the season and the meaning behind it seeped into our family, and we were closer as a result.

We stood together as brothers and sisters at the edge of anticipation, vulnerable, from the eldest to the youngest, holding our emotions in like trapped breath, waiting to see if our silent wishes had been fulfilled. It was the one time of the year where in the midst of many, we all felt the possibility of being recognized as an individual, the possibility of a tiny tap on the shoulder that said, "You are unique to me and I know you." The desire for this magic bordered us, knitting us closer in its suspense.

A red truck. A pair of boots. A doll. Those wishes stood in our midst like a beautiful angel, a presence we somehow sensed but never acknowledged. We basked in its warmth, each with a different wish—all fresh with anticipation.

My parents, shopping at the local department store, tried to remember ages and interests. But with that many children, it was nearly impossible to afford it all, let alone be accurate. Still, they did their best, knowing that since they could only get each child one gift, it had to be close to right.

I awakened on my fifth Christmas sensitive to the mystery surrounding the event. That year, it didn't matter much to me what I received. The feeling of belonging was enough. Christmas morning, long before a decent hour, we stirred one at a time, sleepily making our way down to the tree. What a bounty awaited us. All those presents!

We eagerly tore into the pile, searching for our own names on the packages. I couldn't yet read, so my search was just a scramble for the ignored gifts. I watched as each package was opened until there was only one left. I knew it had to be mine.

Tossing aside tape, bow, and candy cane paper, I eagerly unwrapped a lovely new doll. Just perfect! I didn't remember asking for anything in particular that year, but this was more than I'd ever expected. I cuddled the doll to my chest and sat back, warmed by the "Ooohs" and "Aaahs" of those around me. Resting in the moment of oneness, I watched the rest of the family examining their gifts.

Paul was already driving his red truck through the paper rubble. Laura was joyfully popping the center bubble on the game of Trouble. The older kids were sitting back watching the younger ones. Everyone was caught up in the event. Everyone except my sister Lisa.

Sad. That's how Lisa looked to me as she sat expressionless, holding a stuffed blue dog. Staring into the distance, she seemed lost in another world. Every so often, I'd see her eyes run the length of my doll, and then quickly dart away.

As the last of the paper was cleared away and the living room emptied, Lisa came up behind me.

"Sandy," she started softly, blue dog dangling from her hand, "more than anything, I really wanted a doll for Christmas."

I listened.

"And…" She was eyeing my doll, and I began to understand. I gave the blue dog the once over.

"I was hoping that maybe we could trade?" she ended timidly with a demureness that I recognize now as vulnerability—which in a family as large as mine, could be a critical flaw.

I looked at the doll. Looked down at the blue dog.

"Sure!"

"Really?" Lisa stammered, surprised by my swift response. "You'd trade with me?"

"Mm-hmm," I nodded affirmatively while I watched fresh delight wash across my sister's face.

My arm swung out. The doll landed in a lap of love, and the dog came home to its rightful owner. Its soft fur immediately felt welcome against my skin. The doll looked treasured in Lisa's embrace.

All at once, I received the unexpected, the best gift, the one I'd never asked for but whose offering overwhelmed me then and continues to delight me to this day: Lisa's smile. The doll was not an issue. The dog was not an issue. Lisa's happiness was.

It was a good exchange.

Wild Ride

I don't know what gave him the idea, but somehow my brother got the keys to our family station wagon. He was five and I was four.

"Let's go to the store, Roxanne," he said, as if we did this all the time. I followed behind him, confident in his abilities.

I took Mom's spot in the front passenger seat, he took Dad's behind the wheel, and the journey began. The radio was blaring, and I could see only the sky. Back and forth we drove in the driveway, brakes screeching, car jerking.

The route took us up on the lawn on both sides, over the rock rims that bordered the grass. Howling wildly the entire time, Randy wrestled the car in and out of gear with the enormous shift lever on the steering column. I remember loving the ride as much as the teacups at the Catholic carnival.

The escapade came to a halt when we gently crashed into the stone pillar at the outer end of the blacktop. We were still laughing when the sound of it drove my dad outside to view the debacle.

"Oh, Randy!" Dad's exasperated, thick New York accent bellowed for the entire neighborhood to hear. "Why'dja do that?"

I don't think Dad expected an answer, but Randy gave him one anyway.

"It's fun!" he answered honestly, grinning from ear to ear.

Judging by the look on my father's face, he probably should've lied.

Till Little Arliss got us mixed up in that bear fight, I guess I'd been looking on him about like most boys look on their little brothers. I liked him, all right, but I didn't have a lot of use for him. What with his always playing in our drinking water and getting in the way of my chopping axe and howling his head off and chunking me with rocks when he got mad, it didn't seem to me like he was hardly worth the bother of putting up with. But the day when I saw him in the spring, so helpless against that angry she bear, I learned different. I knew then that I loved him as much as I did Mama and Papa, maybe in some ways even a little bit more.

—Fred Gipson • *Old Yeller*

Perfect Sense

A ministering angel shall my sister be.

—WILLIAM SHAKESPEARE

here was nothing like Zayre's department store in the world— at least not in my world. It seemed like we went to Zayre's nearly every other day. With four kids, our family's list of needs was never ending. As we'd enter the store with Mom through the linen department, my brother, sisters, and I would peer around the kiosks and displays, straining to catch a glimpse of heaven on earth: the toy department.

Walls of toys—cars, dinosaurs, super action heroes, bikes, balls, guns, helmets, swords. It was dizzying. There was never enough time to take it all in. No matter how many hours we spent in there, I always felt cheated when we had to leave, like some new discovery was *just* around the corner.

Mom was usually patient with our pleas to "just look." We were all well behaved, we knew that toys came only on special occasions, we kept our longings silent.

On one special day, we'd finished our shopping for socks and underwear, and we were on our way out of Zayre's.

"Mom, could we go see the toys?" my older sister, Denise, asked.

It was late, but Mom saw the expectant looks on our faces. The nod was given and off we went. Rounding the corner into the superhero section, I stopped dead in my tracks. There in big, bold letters across the front of the aisle hung a huge sign:

Win a Free Toy-Shopping Spree —as much as you can grab!

Crashing into my back as they encountered the sign, my siblings all stood transfixed, carefully reading every jot and tittle, all of us except for my baby sister Holly. She was only four.

"What's it say? What's it say?" she whispered.

"It's a contest, Holly," Denise answered. "It says that if you draw one of the American presidents and your drawing is the best, they'll let you have all the toys you can grab in three minutes."

My jaw hung low. *Wow! All the toys I could grab! A whole three minutes!*

Mom was always talking about what a great artist I was. In

fact, that was all I did lately—draw. Studying each illustration as if it were a Renoir, she would extol the perfectly formed features of Popeye or the exact rendition of Archie. *I was good at this! I knew I could win.*

"How do you enter?" I could barely contain my excitement.

Mom reached up into a small cardboard box affixed to the display, lifting out a few sheets of contest paper. She began to pass them out.

"Jason?" She held one out to my little brother. He shook his head no.

"Denise?"

"No, that's all right, Mom. Jonathan is the artist in the family. Let him try."

Yes! It was in the bag!

"Jonathan? You want to try?" Mom smiled down at me. I felt as if she could hear my shouting thoughts.

"Yes, please." I snatched the paper from her hand.

"Holly?"

Holly? Why is she giving it to Holly? She's just a baby.

"Uh-huh." Holly's long blonde pigtails whipped as her head vigorously bobbed up and down.

Oh, well. She was no competition. What would it hurt? I thought. I had too much to do to worry about little Holly anyway. I had to figure out which president had the most recognizable profile. That's what I could draw best—profiles. Even Mom said so.

Later, at the desk in my room, I glanced at the contest paper:

"On the paper provided, draw a picture of an American president."

And then down at the bottom, I read the most exciting part:

First Prize: A three-minute shopping spree in the toy department.

Second Prize: A three-minute shopping spree in the toy department.

There were also some other prizes, but I didn't pay attention to them. They were for the losers, which I wouldn't be one of.

George Washington? Abraham Lincoln? Thomas Jefferson? I pictured them all in my mind. Which would be the best for my profiling talents? Which would be the most recognizable?

Abe Lincoln. He had a *great* profile. Bumpy and distinct. I moved the overhead lamp into a better position and got to work.

A while later, I emerged from my room. Heart pounding, I ran to find Mom, delicately sandwiching my drawing between my palms so as not to wrinkle it.

I finally found her in the kitchen, glasses perched on the end of her nose, bending over Holly's small body.

"Oh, Holly. It's wonderful! What a great job you did, honey. It looks so much like him." Sensing me behind her, she turned and added, "Let's show it to Jonathan."

Irreverently crumpling her contest paper, Holly's cherubic face quickly lit up with anticipation as she held her illustration out to me.

Indifferently, I took the tiny drawing. I'd used my entire blank space to draw Abe. I wanted the judges to see that I could draw big *and* accurately. That's where Holly's first flaw emerged. Her drawing was less than three inches—total. I saw that right off the bat, even upside down as she handed it to me.

But that wasn't the worst of it. Her drawing was awful! The first thing I thought of was the tiny shriveled apple head dolls we'd seen in the craft store—apples that were left to dry and then painted up to look like old shriveled people. Holly had drawn an old shriveled apple core president with a pig nose—and it looked like it was wearing a wig or something.

"What's *that*?" I asked Mom, stifling my urge to laugh.

Unfazed, smile still holding, she answered, "Why, that's George Washington, Jonathan. Don't you recognize him?"

Taking my cue from her, I examined the drawing more closely. "Oh, I see it now. Yeah, it's George Washington. Is that a wig, Holly?"

"Umm…" She studied her work. "Yeah! It's his white hair." Her grin reminded me that this was just fun for her. I don't think she understood what was truly at stake—*a basket full of toys*—or she would be a little more worried about losing.

"Look at mine, Mom!" I gingerly offered my huge profile for inspection. I watched for a small betrayal in her face. She'd have to be a great actress in front of Holly not to let her see how much better mine was. I looked hard, but it never came.

So much of what is best in us is bound up in our love of family, that it remains the measure of our stability because it measures our sense of loyalty. All other pacts of love or fear derive from it and are modeled upon it.

—Daniel Long

"That's very good, too, Jonathan. You and Holly have both done well. Let's send them in."

That was it? Oh, well. I figured that Mom simply didn't want Holly to lose heart. After all, that apple pig in a wig didn't stand a chance.

A few days later, we were off to Zayre's again. We rushed to the toy department to see if any of the drawings were on display yet.

Holly and I studied the wall where the contest entries hung.

Mine's better…mine's better…mine's better… I walked down the row of drawings, judging each one. A growing excitement rushed me through the last few, only to find that mine wasn't hung yet. Holly's was, and hers looked like one of the worst.

"The contest ends tomorrow," Mom said as she began herding us to the exit. "We'll see what happens."

I wondered for a moment why my drawing wasn't up there. *That's all right*, I thought. *Maybe they're framing the winners or something. They probably held mine back.*

That night in bed, I planned my shopping spree route. First I'd make my way over to the bike aisle, where I'd get a new sparkly seat. Then I'd run to the game section, holding my arm out stiff as I passed through the baseball gloves and bats, just getting whatever fell into my basket—and then… My heart was pounding at the plan.

Late the next afternoon, I was growing more and more nervous. No one had called. I'd asked Mom several times if she was sure this was the day the winners were chosen. She said she was and that I should "Be patient!"

I wasn't.

Holly and I watched "The Flintstones" as we waited. Fred was at the bowling alley with "the boys" when the call came. Holly and I flew into the kitchen, where Mom stood holding the phone, smiling broadly.

"Yes. Yes, we did." She paused, still smiling. "Oh, that is just wonderful! We are so pleased!"

I won! I knew it! I won!

"When? A week from today? Yes, we will be there. Thank you very much!…I will…Thanks, again…Good-bye."

She hung up the phone with great care. All the kids now assembled, still with anticipation. Her eyes fell on each of us as the words began.

"Everyone, we have some wonderful news!"

"What? What? Was it Zayre's? Was it Zayre's?" Jason yelled.

"Yes," to him, and then over to me. "It was Zayre's."

I won. I knew it!

"They called to say that they loved Holly's picture and that she is the grand prize winner! Isn't that great?"

I stared at Holly in amazement. Her full cheeks lifted into an angelic smile. There was a surety about it, as if it all made perfect sense to her. Of course! She'd thought she was going to win, too.

And she had!

"I won! I won!" she squealed as she jumped up and down, pigtails bouncing.

The family swarmed her with hugs, kisses, and congratulations. I stood back, stung by the truth, stunned by the error of it all. How could that pig wig picture have beaten my perfect profile?

I searched frantically for any possible explanation. Maybe the post office never delivered my entry. Maybe someone had misplaced it. Maybe…

All I know is it should've been me! I should've won!

"Isn't it, honey?" Mom's voice broke through my thoughts. "What a wonderful thing for Holly, Jonathan." She touched the side of my face.

"Is that all they said, Mom? Did they say anything else?" I had to know the truth.

"No, hon, that was all they said. Isn't that nice for your sister?" she guided.

"Yea. Congratulations, Holly," I offered half-heartedly as I gave her a pat on the back. But she was lost in the excitement of it all and didn't sense my immense disappointment.

I turned and walked toward my room. I just couldn't believe it. There must have been some mistake. I should've won! My picture was the best.

The next day we went to Zayre's to see Holly's picture hung in the front window, right below the big blue ribbon with gold lettering on it that read: *Grand Prize Winner: First Place.*

The ribbon was bigger than the pig head! And under Holly's picture hung the second-prize winner's okay drawing of Thomas Jefferson by some kid a little younger than me.

We visited the toy department once again on the way out. I was sad and a little bitter. This time we wandered its aisles all together, dreaming in one big group.

"If I'd won, I would've got this," Denise longingly exhaled as she fondled a life-size Barbie doll head, the kind that you could make up and change hairstyles on.

"What about you, Jonathan? What did you want to get?" Mom gently asked.

As if condemned to death, I slid my feet over to Superman. "I wanted this," I said flatly. *If they only knew how much I really would've gotten.*

"Me, too!" chimed in Jason. "I like that guy, too!"

Holly stood by smiling. She was too little to strategize, but I was sure she had a few favorites in mind. She never pointed out what they were, but we'd all see next Saturday when she had her three minutes.

I tried not to think about it all week long. Every time it came into my mind, I would just tell myself that it was a mistake and there was nothing I could do about it. Next time—if there ever was a next time—I would bring my drawing in person and give it to the lady at the cash register. Forget the mail.

It is more blessed to give than to receive.
—The Book of Acts

The next Saturday Zayre's was packed with people, all there to see the sweep. The same smile that had held on Holly's face followed her to the starting line. She was just happy to be there. It was enough.

The second-prize winner was a boy much bigger than Holly. He already stood poised, fingers twitching on the grip bar of the shopping cart in front of him. Holly was too small to reach her grip, so the storeowner approached Dad. Moments later, Denise stood behind a cart at Holly's side. She would push while Holly grabbed.

Like some grand sporting event, the crowd hushed and tensed as the rules were announced.

"Three minutes total…anything you can get into the basket…good luck, winners!"

"On your mark, get set…" The storeowner held the stopwatch high, one side of his suit jacket gently swaying from the motion. "…go!"

And off my two sisters went, amidst screams and cheers, banking the first corner and disappearing into the stacks of hard plastic swimming pools.

"Go, Holly! Go, Denise! Atta girl!" my family screamed. People around us joined in, too, whistling and clapping.

"You can do it!" Dad called loudly.

They came around corner number three in a blur. I couldn't make out what Holly had grabbed, but I could see her chubby red face. Little arms pumping, tiny legs in a patter of baby steps, she swung into the next aisle, smiling all the while.

She looked so happy. Somehow it made it almost all right.

"Go, Holly!" I yelled. Mom turned toward me, catching my eye. She smiled.

"You can do it, Holly!" I yelled, for real this time.

The crowd continued to whistle and clap. The other boy had so much in his basket that it was falling over the sides. He chose a lot of the stuff I would've got. He couldn't seem to keep it all in.

The storeowner began counting over the crowd.

"Five…four…three…two…one!" A whistle blew and Holly, with Denise in tow, rounded the last corner and headed toward us. Her basket wasn't nearly as full as the other kid's was. In fact, it looked kind of empty.

"I got it all!" she beamed as she came to a stop in front of us, puffing the words out.

I approached the basket for a better look at the contents. What I saw stunned me.

A life-size Barbie doll head. Two Superman action figures. A tiny doll. Nothing more.

Holly stepped up on the lower part of the basket and precariously dangled over its side, reaching for the first item. The Barbie head went to Denise.

"Thanks, Holly!" Denise kissed her little sister's cheek as she took the huge box from Holly's grip.

"You're welcome." Holly climbed up to get one of the Superman figures. Teetering on her hip, her tiny fingers grabbed the edge of the long, slender box. Dad helped her down.

"Here, Jason." Holly was still smiling.

"Wow! Thanks, Holly!" It was Christmas to Jason. He didn't expect it was for him even when he saw it in the cart.

Back into the cart Holly went, and I felt a mixture of excitement and guilt. She teetered on the metal rim, catching the second Superman box on her fingernail.

"Here, Jonathan," she grunted as Dad helped her down. "This is for you." She held the box out to me with both hands, Superman facing me with his arms raised for flight.

"Thank you, Holly," I said as I took the box from her grasp. She followed it with a hug on my side, burying her smiling face into my waist.

Pulling back, she reached for Dad's hand. He placed her new doll in the crook of her free arm.

"Let's go now!" Her smile never wavered as she started pulling Dad along.

It all made perfect sense to her, and as we walked away, I noticed the crowd watching us leave. Even the boy with everything I wanted paused to look on. I looked back at him with his basket and I didn't feel sad. I turned forward to see the back of Holly's baby legs wobbling in front of me as she held Dad's grip, and I knew it was all meant to be.

I was glad she won. *It should've been her*, I thought, and I knew it was true.